beaded bracelets
to KNIT

Each of these 15 exciting bracelet designs gives you the opportunity to add more color and sparkle to your life—with knitting! Using embroidery floss and beads, you can knit the bracelets as shown, or change the floss and bead colors to create jewelry that's uniquely yours. We have included Bracelet Basics to help you with knitting with polyester floss, choosing the best bead size, and how adding closures will help you get an even, professional finish. You'll also see how easy it is to add charms to your bracelet. And by following the instructions for pattern variations, you can custom-fit these designs for any size wrist. What lovely gifts to make for your friends or yourself!

LEISURE ARTS, INC.
Little Rock, Arkansas

BRACELET BASICS

Before beginning to knit these bracelets, it is best to familiarize yourself with the following tips and techniques.

Each pattern shows you how to make a different type of bracelet. Using the same pattern, you can create your own designs by simply changing the colors, bead size, or width of the bracelet. You can also apply a different finishing technique or closure.

GAUGE

Gauge is not essential in these patterns. After knitting a few rows, you will be able to measure your own gauge and customize the size of your bracelet by determining the length of a pattern repeat. For example, if one pattern repeat equals half an inch, you can adjust the size of your bracelet in half-inch increments by adding or subtracting one pattern repeat. This will vary from bracelet to bracelet because of the size of the beads and the number of knitted rows in the repeat. The patterns are written to fit wrist sizes $7^1/_4$-$7^3/_4$" (18.5-20 cm). Periodically measure the bracelet fabric around your wrist to determine your correct size. Remember to take into account that the toggle closure will add another 1-$1^1/_2$" (2.5-4 cm) to the finished size.

It is important to work with consistent, firm tension throughout the patterns. Working too loosely will produce a sloppy look, while working too tightly will make the stitches difficult to work. When starting a new row, gently tug the first one or two stitches to firm the tension. This helps add shape to the edging, creating a slight cuff along the edge. Additionally, the knitted fabric acts as a support to the bead work. Check your work every few rows for consistent tension and proper bead placement.

KNITTING NEEDLES

Polyester floss moves most easily on bamboo knitting needles. If you find the floss too slippery to work with, try again with plastic or acrylic knitting needles. Tug slightly on the floss to tighten stitches at the beginning and end of a row. Tightening the edge stitches can make them more difficult to work. In this case, work the stitches at the tip of the needle. Take care to work slowly and carefully to prevent accidentally slipping stitches off the needles.

KNITTING WITH EMBROIDERY FLOSS

The bracelets in this book are knit with 6-ply polyester metallic embroidery floss. When working with embroidery floss, you will be working with all the plies held together. Make sure you catch all plies into each stitch when working a stitch. This will help you avoid having any loose or stray threads in your bracelet. Check your work frequently. If you happen to miss any threads and are well into your knitting, stitch them down with matching sewing thread at the completion of the bracelet.

Like many knitting yarns, metallic floss will sometimes kink or twist. A kink is usually just a slip knot that forms in the floss. If this happens, take a blunt needle and insert it into the knot. This will usually loosen it enough to release. If the floss twists while working, allow it to dangle periodically to unwind (as you would do with a coiled telephone cord).

Before sewing or restringing beads, cut away any frayed ends. You will have ample floss to cut away a bit of fray if you leave the suggested tail length when casting on and binding off.

The patterns call for more floss than you are likely to use. The wider bracelet designs require 2 or 3 skeins to complete and will support a knot that can easily be hidden in the back of the knitted fabric. Some patterns will not support a knot since there is no place to hide one in the finished product. Therefore, it is always wise to start each project with a new skein of floss.

JOINING NEW FLOSS

When attaching a new skein of floss in the middle of the project, stop at least 6" (15 cm) from the end of the old floss on a non-beaded row. String additional beads needed on your new floss before joining the floss together so that the beads on your new floss will be in position for the next beaded row. Join the floss together with an overhand knot and continue knitting the remainder of the row. Don't worry if the knot falls to the front of your work. When your bracelet is complete, pull the knot to the back and stitch it down to the bracelet fabric with matching sewing thread. Cut the excess floss away close to the wrong side of your work, then reinforce with clear nail polish.

WORKING WITH BEADS

In most cases, each bead sits between two stitches. This is accomplished by sliding the bead into place before knitting or purling the next stitch. Be sure not to work the bead into the actual stitch. Slide each bead into place and hold it against the knitted fabric, then knit or purl the next stitch making sure that your floss comes up **over** the bead, not **under** it. When placing beads on a knit row, the bead will fall behind your work. Conversely, when adding beads on a purl row, the bead will fall to the front of your work.

BEADING NEEDLE

You can thread your beads with a purchased beading needle, or you can make your own beading needle. To make your own beading needle, thread regular sewing thread through a thin-eyed sewing needle, double the thread and tie a small knot approximately 2" (5 cm) from the eye of the needle. Slip your floss through the thread loop, then use the needle to pick up the beads and slip them over the thread and onto the floss.

CHOOSING BEADS

There are many different beads to choose from. Size 6/0, 6°, or size E seed beads all describe the same size bead and are the smallest size bead that will fit over the floss comfortably. Glass beads in lengths of 4, 6, 8 and 10 mm work well with the projects in this leaflet. You may also wish to incorporate a few charms or leaf, flower, or teardrop beads into your bracelets. These work well in the Forest Whispers and Ocean Breeze bracelet patterns. Check to see that the beads you want to use have a large enough hole for the floss to pass through.

Several patterns call for spacer beads. Spacer beads have larger holes and are used between the end of the bracelet and the toggle clasp. Their holes must be large enough for the floss to pass through at least twice.

STRINGING BEADS

Each pattern requires stringing the beads onto your floss, either randomly or in a set pattern. The last bead strung will be the first bead you will use. If you have extra beads on your floss when your knitting reaches your desired length, the extra beads can easily be removed from your floss. If, by chance, you run out of beads before your knitting is complete, you can add more beads to the opposite end of your floss, taking care to follow the proper stringing order if following a particular stringing sequence. Stringing beads from the opposite end means that the first bead strung will be the first bead used. While stringing your beads, gently guide them down the floss in small groups to prevent fraying. Slide the beads far enough down onto the floss to allow slack for casting on and knitting your first few stitches. Do not wind beaded floss, as it will tangle. Allow it to drop into your lap or into a bowl or basket.

spacers

toggle

RAINBOW

Skill Level: ◖■◻▢ **EASY**

Finished Size: $1^1/_2$" (4 cm) wide x $7^1/_4$" (18.5 cm) long (including toggle); Bracelet will stretch to fit $7^1/_4$-$7^3/_4$" wrist (18.5-20 cm)

MATERIALS
- Polyester embroidery floss, $8^3/_4$ yards (8 meters) - 2 skeins
- Straight knitting needles, size 2 (2.75 mm)
- Assorted 4-10 mm glass beads - 108
- Spacer beads - 2
- Toggle clasp set
- Blunt tapestry needle
- Beading needle
- Sewing needle and thread to match floss
- Clear nail polish

To lengthen or shorten by $^3/_8$" (1 cm), increase or decrease the number of beads strung in increments of 7.

Bracelet
String Beads: Using beading needle, string 80 beads onto floss in random order.

Leaving a 24" (61 cm) end, cast on 9 sts.

Rows 1-3: Knit across.

Row 4 (Right side)**:** K2, WYF slide bead up, P1, ★ K1, WYF slide bead up , P1; repeat from ★ across to last 2 sts, K2: 3 beads.

Row 5: Knit across.

Row 6: K1, ★ WYF slide bead up, P1, K1; repeat from ★ across: 4 beads.

Row 7: Knit across.

Repeat Rows 4-7 for pattern until you reach the end of your floss, ending by working Row 6. String 28 beads onto second strand of floss. With first floss, knit to the middle of the row, join second skein and knit across **(see Joining New Floss, page 3)**.

Continue in pattern until Bracelet measures approximately $5^3/_4$" (14.5 cm) from cast on edge or $1^1/_2$" (4 cm) less than desired finished length, ending by working Row 5.

Last 2 Rows: Knit across.

Bind off all sts. Cut floss leaving a 24" (61 cm) end.

FINISHING
Thread tapestry needle with end and work blanket stitch across bound off stitches to reinforce edge **(Figs. 1a & b, page 34)**. Weave end to center of short edge. ★ Remove tapestry needle and thread beading needle with end. Pass through spacer bead, through toggle, then back through spacer bead allowing $^1/_4$" (6 mm) slack on each side of toggle. Remove beading needle and thread tapestry needle with end. Knot securely at center of short edge. Repeat from ★ once **more** taking care not to catch previous floss when passing through spacer bead. Cut floss leaving a $^1/_{16}$" (1.5 mm) end. Anchor end with matching sewing thread. Apply clear nail polish to end and tuck end inside spacer bead.

Repeat for second end.

Pattern Variations: This Bracelet can be worked with any odd number of sts. For a narrower Bracelet cast on 5 or 7 sts and adjust the number of beads strung accordingly; for a wider Bracelet, cast on 11 or 13 sts.

PINK ICE CUFF

Skill Level: ◖■□□ **EASY**

Finished Size: 1¹/₂" (4 cm) wide x 7¹/₄" (18.5 cm) long (including toggle); Bracelet will stretch to fit 7¹/₄-7³/₄" wrist (18.5-20 cm)

MATERIALS
Polyester embroidery floss, 8³/₄ yards (8 meters) - 2 skeins
Straight knitting needles, size 2 (2.75 mm)
Assorted 4-10 mm glass beads - 108
Toggle clasp set
Blunt tapestry needle
Beading needle
Sewing needle and thread to match floss
Clear nail polish

To lengthen or shorten by ³/₈" (1 cm), increase or decrease the number of beads strung in increments of 7.

Bracelet
String Beads: Using beading needle, string 80 beads onto floss in random order.

Leaving a 24" (61 cm) end, cast on 9 sts.

Rows 1-3: Knit across.

Row 4: (Right side)**:** K2, WYF slide bead up, P1, ★ K1, WYF slide bead up , P1; repeat from ★ across to last 2 sts, K2: 3 beads.

Row 5: Knit across.

Row 6: K1, ★ WYF slide bead up, P1, K1; repeat from ★ across: 4 beads.

Row 7: Knit across.

Repeat Rows 4-7 for pattern until you reach the end of your floss, ending by working Row 6. String 28 beads onto second strand of floss. With first floss, knit to the middle of the row, join second skein and knit across *(see Joining New Floss, page 3)*.

Continue in pattern until Bracelet measures approximately 5³/₄" (14.5 cm) from cast on edge or 1¹/₂" (4 cm) less than desired finished length, ending by working Row 5.

Last 2 Rows: Knit across.

Bind off all sts. Cut floss leaving a 24" (61 cm) end.

FINISHING
Thread tapestry needle with end and work blanket stitch across bound off stitches to reinforce edge *(Figs. 1a & b, page 34)*. Weave end to center of short edge, then thread end through toggle. Allowing ¹/₄" (6 mm) slack on each side of toggle, secure tightly to Bracelet edge with a knot. Cut floss leaving a ¹/₁₆" (1.5 mm) end. Anchor end with matching sewing thread. Apply clear nail polish to end.

Repeat for second end.

Pattern Variations: This Bracelet can be worked with any odd number of sts. For a narrower Bracelet cast on 5 or 7 sts and adjust the number of beads strung accordingly; for a wider Bracelet, cast on 11 or 13 sts.

TWILIGHT

Skill Level: ■■□□ **EASY**

Finished Size: $1/2$" (12 mm) wide x $7^1/4$" (18.5 cm) long (including toggle); Bracelet will stretch to fit $7^1/4$-$7^3/4$" wrist (18.5-20 cm)

MATERIALS
Polyester embroidery floss, $8^3/4$ yards (8 meters) - 1 skein
Straight knitting needles, size 2 (2.75 mm)
Assorted 4-6 mm glass seed beads - 232
Spacer beads - 2
Toggle clasp set
Blunt tapestry needle
Beading needle
Sewing needle and thread to match floss
Clear nail polish

To lengthen or shorten by $3/8$" (1 cm), increase or decrease the number of beads strung in increments of 15.

Bracelet
String Beads: Using beading needle, string 232 beads onto floss in random order.

Leaving a 16" (41 cm) end, cast on 4 sts.

Rows 1 and 2: Knit across.

Row 3 (Right side)**:** WYB slide bead up, ★ K1, WYF slide 3 beads up, P1; repeat from ★ across: 7 beads.

Row 4: WYB slide bead up, knit across.

Row 5: ★ WYF slide 3 beads up, P1, K1; repeat from ★ across: 6 beads.

Row 6: WYB slide bead up, knit across.

Repeat Rows 3-6 for pattern until Bracelet measures approximately $5^3/4$" (14.5 cm) from cast on edge or $1^1/2$" (4 cm) less than desired finished length, ending by working Row 3.

Last Row: Knit across.

Bind off all sts. Cut floss leaving a 24" (61 cm) end.

FINISHING
Thread tapestry needle with end and work blanket stitch across bound off stitches to reinforce edge *(Figs. 1a & b, page 34)*. Weave end to center of short edge. ★ Remove tapestry needle and thread beading needle with end. Pass through spacer bead, through toggle, then back through spacer bead allowing $1/4$" (6 mm) slack on each side of toggle. Remove beading needle and thread tapestry needle with end. Knot securely at center of short edge. Repeat from ★ once **more** taking care not to catch previous floss when passing through spacer bead. Cut floss leaving a $1/16$" (1.5 mm) end. Anchor end with matching sewing thread. Apply clear nail polish to end and tuck end inside spacer bead.

Repeat for second end.

Pattern Variations: This Bracelet can be worked with any even number of sts. For a wider Bracelet cast on 6, 8, 10 or 12 sts and adjust the number of beads strung accordingly.

CRYSTAL LAKE

Skill Level: ■■□□ **EASY**

Finished Size: 1¹/₄" (3 cm) wide x 7¹/₄" (18.5 cm) long (including toggle); Bracelet will stretch to fit 7¹/₄-7³/₄" wrist (18.5-20 cm)

MATERIALS
Polyester embroidery floss, 8³/₄ yards (8 meters) - 1 skein
Straight knitting needles, size 2 (2.75 mm)
4 mm Glass cube beads - 16
6 mm Oval beads - 84
Toggle clasp set
Blunt tapestry needle
Beading needle
Sewing needle and thread to match floss
Clear nail polish

To lengthen or shorten by ¹/₄" (6 mm), increase or decrease the number of larger beads strung in increments of 4.

Bracelet
String Beads: Using beading needle, string 8 cube beads, string 84 oval beads, string 8 cube beads.

Leaving a 16" (41 cm) tail, cast on 7 sts.

Rows 1 and 2: Knit across.

Row 3: K2, WYB slide bead up, ★ K1, WYB slide bead up; repeat from ★ across to last 2 sts, K2: 4 beads.

Row 4 (Right side)**:** Purl across.

Repeat Rows 3 and 4 for pattern until Bracelet measures approximately 5¹/₂" (14 cm) from cast on edge or 1³/₄" (4.5 cm) less than desired finished length, all larger beads are used, and ending by working Row 4.

Next 3 Rows: Repeat Rows 3 and 4 once, then repeat Row 3 once **more**.

Last Row: Knit across.

Bind off all sts. Cut floss leaving a 16" (41 cm) end.

FINISHING
Thread tapestry needle with end and work blanket stitch across bound off stitches to reinforce edge *(Figs. 1a & b, page 34)*. Weave end to center of short edge, then thread end through toggle. Allowing ¹/₄" (6 mm) slack on each side of toggle, secure tightly to Bracelet edge with a knot. Cut floss leaving a ¹/₁₆" (1.5 mm) end. Anchor end with matching sewing thread. Apply clear nail polish to end.

Repeat for second end.

Pattern Variations: This Bracelet can be worked with any odd number of sts. For a narrower Bracelet cast on 5 sts and adjust the number of beads strung accordingly; for a wider Bracelet, cast on 9 or 11 sts.

BEADS GALORE

Skill Level: ⬛⬛◻◻ **EASY**

Finished Size: 1½" (4 cm) wide x 7¼" (18.5 cm) long (including toggle); Bracelet will stretch to fit 7¼-7¾" wrist (18.5-20 cm)

MATERIALS
Polyester embroidery floss, 8¾ yards (8 meters) - 1 skein
Straight knitting needles, sizes 2 (2.75 mm) **and** 5 (3.75 mm)
4 mm Round beads - 16
8 mm Round beads - 60
Toggle clasp set
Blunt tapestry needle
Beading needle
Sewing needle and thread to match floss
Clear nail polish

To lengthen or shorten by ³⁄₈" (1 cm), increase or decrease the number of larger beads strung in increments of 4.

Bracelet
String Beads: Using beading needle, string 8 smaller beads, string 60 larger beads, string 8 smaller beads.

With smaller size needles, and leaving a 16" (41 cm) tail, cast on 7 sts.

Rows 1 and 2: Knit across.

Row 3: K2, WYB slide bead up, ★ K1, WYB slide bead up; repeat from ★ across to last 2 sts, K2: 4 beads.

Row 4 (Right side)**:** Purl across.

Rows 5 and 6: Repeat Rows 3 and 4.

Change to larger size needles.

Repeat Rows 3 and 4 for pattern until Bracelet measures approximately 5¼" (13.5 cm) from cast on edge or 2" (5 cm) less than desired finished length, all larger beads are used, and ending by working Row 4.

Change to smaller size needles.

Next 3 Rows: Repeat Rows 3 and 4 once, then repeat Row 3 once **more**.

Last Row: Knit across.

Bind off all sts. Cut floss leaving a 16" (41 cm) end.

FINISHING
Thread tapestry needle with end and work blanket stitch across bound off stitches to reinforce edge **(Figs. 1a & b, page 34)**. Weave end to center of short edge, then thread end through toggle. Allowing ¼" (6 mm) slack on each side of toggle, secure tightly to Bracelet edge with a knot. Cut floss leaving a ¹⁄₁₆" (1.5 mm) end. Anchor end with matching sewing thread. Apply clear nail polish to end.

Repeat for second end.

Pattern Variations: This Bracelet can be worked with any odd number of sts. For a narrower Bracelet cast on 5 sts and adjust the number of beads accordingly; for a wider Bracelet, cast on 9 or 11 sts.

DAZZLE BRAID

Skill Level: ⬤⬤◻◻ **EASY**

Finished Size: 1" (2.5 cm) wide x 7$\frac{1}{4}$" (18.5 cm) long (including toggle); Bracelet will stretch to fit 7$\frac{1}{4}$-7$\frac{3}{4}$" wrist (18.5-20 cm)

MATERIALS
Polyester embroidery floss, 8$\frac{3}{4}$ yards (8 meters)
- 1 skein of Color A and 1 skein of Color B
Straight knitting needles, size 2 (2.75 mm)
Glass seed beads - 102
4 mm Glass cube beads - 49
Spacer beads - 2
Toggle clasp set
Blunt tapestry needle
Beading needle
Sewing needle and thread to match floss
Clear nail polish

The size of the Bracelet is determined by the number of cast on sts. To lengthen or shorten by $\frac{1}{2}$" (12 mm), increase or decrease the number of cast on sts in increments of 3, and adjust the number of beads strung accordingly.

Bracelet
FIRST STRAND
String Beads: Using beading needle, string 38 seed beads onto floss Color A.

Leaving a 16" (41 cm) end, cast on 39 sts.

Row 1: K1, ★ slide bead up, K1, pass first st on right needle over second st and off needle; repeat from ★ across.

Cut floss leaving a 16" (41 cm) end.

SECOND STRAND
Work same as First Strand using floss Color B.

THIRD STRAND
String Beads: Using beading needle, string 36 cube beads onto floss Color B.

Leaving a 16" (41 cm) end, cast on 37 sts.

Complete same as First Strand.

FOURTH STRAND
String Beads: Using beading needle and floss Color A, string one seed bead, string one cube bead, ★ string two seed beads, string one cube bead; repeat from ★ 11 times **more**, string one seed bead.

Leaving a 16" (41 cm) end, cast on 40 sts.

Complete same as First Strand.

FINISHING
FIRST END
Holding 4 ends together, tie an overhand knot snugly against the end of all strands. Using beading needle, thread ends through spacer bead. Make a second overhand knot approximately $\frac{1}{2}$" (12 mm) from first knot. Insert ends through ring of the bar side of toggle clasp, then tie a third overhand knot, leaving a $\frac{1}{4}$" (6 mm) of slack on each side of the toggle. Thread ends back through spacer bead. Remove beading needle and thread tapestry needle, then knot the ends securely to the strands. Cut floss leaving $\frac{1}{16}$" (1.5 mm) ends. Anchor ends with matching sewing thread. Apply clear nail polish to ends and overhand knots.

Tape the finished end to a solid surface. Using medium braiding tension and holding the First and Third Strands together as a single unit, braid the strands together, taking care to keep bead sides facing and stretching gently so that all cords are the same length at the bottom edge. Tie an overhand knot securing the bottom ends together. The braid will gently loosen as you tie the bottom.

SECOND END
Thread beading needle with ends. Pass through spacer bead, through toggle, then back through spacer bead allowing $1/4$" (6 mm) slack on each side of toggle. Remove beading needle and thread tapestry needle with end. Knot securely to end of strands. Cut floss leaving a $1/16$" (1.5 mm) end. Anchor ends with matching sewing thread. Apply clear nail polish to ends.

Pattern Variations: Work a 3-strand braid for a slightly narrower Bracelet or work 2 strands and twist together, serpentine style.

PURPLE PASSION BANGLE

Skill Level: ⬤▨☐☐ **EASY**

Finished Size: $3/4$" (2 cm) wide x $7^1/4$" (18.5 cm) long (including toggle); Bracelet will stretch to fit $7^1/4$-$7^3/4$" wrist (18.5-20 cm)

MATERIALS
Polyester embroidery floss, $8^3/4$ yards (8 meters)
  - 2 skeins
Straight knitting needles, size 2 (2.75 mm)
Assorted glass seed beads - 204
Spacer beads - 2
Toggle clasp set
Blunt tapestry needle
Beading needle
Sewing needle and thread to match floss
Clear nail polish

To lengthen or shorten by $3/8$" (1 cm), increase or decrease the number of beads strung in increments of 12.

Bracelet
String Beads: Using beading needle, string 204 beads onto floss in random order.

Leaving a 16" (41 cm) end, cast on 9 sts.

Rows 1-4: Knit across.

Row 5 (Wrong side)**:** K2, WYB slide 2 beads up, ★ K1, WYB slide 2 beads up; repeat from ★ across to last 2 sts, K2: 12 beads.

Rows 6-8: Knit across.

Repeat Rows 5-8 for pattern until Bracelet measures approximately $5^3/4$" (14.5 cm) from cast on edge or $1^1/2$" (4 cm) less than desired finished length, ending by working Row 8.

Bind off all sts. Cut floss leaving a 24" (61 cm) end.

FINISHING
FIRST END
Fold Bracelet in half lengthwise with wrong sides together. Thread tapestry needle with long end and sew short edge together. Weave end to center of short end. ★ Remove tapestry needle and thread beading needle with end. Pass through spacer bead, through toggle, then back through spacer bead allowing $1/4$" (6 mm) slack on each side of toggle. Remove beading needle and thread tapestry needle with end. Knot securely at center of short edge. Repeat from ★ once **more** taking care not to catch previous floss when passing through spacer bead. With same end, weave long edges together **(Fig. 2, page 34)**, ending at opposite short end. Secure end tightly with a knot. Cut floss leaving a $1/16$" (1.5 mm) end. Anchor end with matching sewing thread. Apply clear nail polish to end.

SECOND END
Thread tapestry needle with cast on end and sew short edge together. Weave end to center of short end. ★ Remove tapestry needle and thread beading needle with end. Pass through spacer bead, through toggle, then back through spacer bead allowing $1/4$" (6 mm) slack on each side of toggle. Remove beading needle and thread tapestry needle with end. Knot securely at center of short edge. Repeat from ★ once **more** taking care not to catch previous floss when passing through spacer bead. Cut floss leaving a $1/16$" (1.5 mm) end. Anchor end with matching sewing thread. Apply clear nail polish to end and tuck end inside spacer bead.

GOLDEN SEA

Skill Level: ⬤◼◻◻ **EASY**

Finished Size: 1¼" (3 cm) wide x 7¼" (18.5 cm) long (including joining); Bracelet will stretch to fit 7¼"-7¾" wrist (18.5-20 cm)

MATERIALS
- Polyester embroidery floss, 8¾ yards (8 meters) - 1 skein
- Straight knitting needles, size 2 (2.75 mm)
- Assorted 4-6 mm glass seed beads - 403
- ¾" (2 cm) Oval bead for closure - 1
- Blunt tapestry needle
- Beading needle
- Sewing needle and thread to match floss
- Clear nail polish

To lengthen or shorten by ½" (12 mm), increase or decrease the number of beads strung in increments of 27.

Bracelet
String Beads: Using beading needle, string 391 beads onto floss in random order.

Leaving a 16" (41 cm) end, cast on 8 sts.

Rows 1 and 2: Knit across.

Row 3 (Right side)**:** WYB slide bead up, ★ K1, WYF slide 3 beads up, P1; repeat from ★ across: 13 beads.

Row 4: WYB slide bead up, knit across.

Row 5: ★ WYF slide 3 beads up, P1, K1; repeat from ★ across: 12 beads.

Row 6: WYB slide bead up, knit across.

Repeat Rows 3-6 for pattern until Bracelet measures approximately 5¾" (14.5 cm) from cast on edge or 1½" (4 cm) less than desired finished length, ending by working Row 3.

Last Row: Knit across.

Bind off all sts. Cut floss leaving a 24" (61 cm) end.

FINISHING
FIRST END
Thread tapestry needle with end and work blanket stitch across bound off stitches to reinforce edge *(**Figs. 1a & b, page 34**)*. Weave end to ⅜" (1 cm) from edge. Remove tapestry needle and thread beading needle with end. String remaining 12 beads onto floss. Form loop with remaining beads and knot securely ⅜" (1 cm) from opposite edge. Cut floss leaving a 1/16" (1.5 mm) end. Anchor end with matching sewing thread. Apply clear nail polish to end.

SECOND END
Thread tapestry needle with beginning end and work blanket stitch across cast on stitches to reinforce edge. Thread end through large oval bead, and knot tightly at opposite edge. Cut floss leaving a 1/16" (1.5 mm) end. Anchor end with matching sewing thread. Apply clear nail polish to end.

Pattern Variations: This Bracelet can be worked with any even number of sts. For a narrower Bracelet cast on 4 or 6 sts and adjust the number of beads strung accordingly; for a wider Bracelet, cast on 10 or 12 sts.

FIRE AND ICE

Skill Level: ▭■▭▭ **EASY**

Finished Size: $1/2$" (12 mm) wide x $7^1/2$" (19 cm) long (including toggle); Bracelet will stretch to fit $7^1/2$-$7^3/4$" wrist (19-20 cm)

MATERIALS

Polyester embroidery floss, $8^3/4$ yards (8 meters) – 1 skein
Straight knitting needles, size 2 (2.75 mm)
6 mm Glass beads: Color A - 30; Color B - 29
6 mm Spacer beads - 2
Toggle clasp set
Blunt tapestry needle
Beading needle
Sewing needle and thread
Clear nail polish

To lengthen or shorten by $1/4$" (6 mm), increase or decrease the number of beads strung in increments of 2.

Bracelet

String Beads: Using beading needle, string one Color A bead, ★ string one Color B bead, string one Color A bead; repeat from ★ until all beads have been strung.

Leaving a 16" (41 cm) end, cast on 2 sts.

Rows 1 and 2: Knit across.

Row 3: K1, WYF slide bead up, P1.

Repeat Row 3 for pattern until Bracelet measures approximately 6" (15 cm) from cast on edge or $1^1/2$" (4 cm) less than desired finished length, ending by placing a Color A bead.

Last 2 Rows: Knit across.

Bind off all sts. Cut floss leaving a 16" (41 cm) end.

FINISHING

Thread tapestry needle with end and work blanket stitch across bound off stitches to reinforce edge **(Figs. 1a & b, page 34)**. Weave end to center of short edge. ★ Remove tapestry needle and thread beading needle with end. Pass through spacer bead, through toggle, then back through spacer bead allowing $1/4$" (6 mm) slack on each side of toggle. Remove beading needle and thread tapestry needle with end. Knot securely at center of short edge. Repeat from ★ once **more** taking care not to catch previous floss when passing through spacer bead. Cut floss leaving a $1/16$" (1.5 mm) end. Anchor end with matching sewing thread. Apply clear nail polish to end and tuck end inside spacer bead.

Repeat for second end.

HOT PASTEL GUM DROPS

Skill Level: ⬤■☐☐ **EASY**

Finished Size: $3/4$" (2 cm) wide x $7^1/4$" (18.5 cm) long (including toggle); Bracelet will stretch to fit $7^1/4$-$7^3/4$" wrist (18.5-20 cm)

MATERIALS
- Polyester embroidery floss, $8^3/4$ yards (8 meters) - 1 skein
- Straight knitting needles, size 2 (2.75 mm)
- Assorted 4-10 mm glass beads - 30
- Spacer beads - 2
- Toggle clasp set
- Blunt tapestry needle
- Beading needle
- Sewing needle and thread to match floss
- Clear nail polish

To lengthen or shorten by $3/8$" (1 cm), increase or decrease the number of beads strung in increments of 2.

Bracelet
String Beads: Using beading needle, string 30 beads onto floss in random order.

Leaving a 16" (41 cm) end, cast on 3 sts.

Rows 1 and 2: Knit across.

Row 3 (Right side)**:** K1, WYF slide bead up, P1, K1.

Row 4: Knit across.

Row 5: K2, WYF slide bead up, P1.

Row 6: Knit across.

Repeat Rows 3-6 for pattern until Bracelet measures approximately $5^3/4$" (14.5 cm) from cast on edge or $1^1/2$" (4 cm) less than desired finished length, ending by working Row 6.

Last Row: Knit across.

Bind off all sts. Cut floss leaving a 16" (41 cm) end.

FINISHING
Thread tapestry needle with end and work blanket stitch across bound off stitches to reinforce edge *(Figs. 1a & b, page 34)*. Weave end to center of short edge. ★ Remove tapestry needle and thread beading needle with end. Pass through spacer bead, through toggle, then back through spacer bead allowing $1/4$" (6 mm) slack on each side of toggle. Remove beading needle and thread tapestry needle with end. Knot securely at center of short edge. Repeat from ★ once **more** taking care not to catch previous floss when passing through spacer bead. Cut floss leaving a $1/16$" (1.5 mm) end. Anchor end with matching sewing thread. Apply clear nail polish to end and tuck end inside spacer bead.

Repeat for second end.

YOUR CHOICE

Skill Level: ⬤◼◻◻ **EASY**

Finished Size: $3/4$" (2 cm) wide x $7^1/4$" (18.5 cm) long (including toggle); Bracelet will stretch to fit $7^1/4$-$7^3/4$" wrist (18.5-20 cm)

MATERIALS
- Polyester embroidery floss, $8^3/4$ yards (8 meters) - 1 skein
- Straight knitting needles, size 2 (2.75 mm)
- Assorted 4-10 mm glass beads - 31
- Spacer beads - 2
- Toggle clasp set
- Blunt tapestry needle
- Beading needle
- Sewing needle and thread to match floss
- Clear nail polish

To lengthen or shorten by $3/8$" (1 cm), increase or decrease the number of beads strung in increments of 2.

Bracelet
String Beads: Using beading needle, string 31 beads onto floss in random order.

Leaving a 16" (41 cm) end, cast on 3 sts.

Rows 1 and 2: Knit across.

Row 3 (Right side)**:** K1, WYF slide bead up, P1, K1.

Row 4: Knit across.

Row 5: K2, WYF slide bead up, P1.

Row 6: Knit across.

Repeat Rows 3-6 for pattern until Bracelet measures approximately $5^3/4$" (14.5 cm) from cast on edge or $1^1/2$" (4 cm) less than desired finished length, ending by working Row 4.

Last Row: Knit across.

Bind off all sts. Cut floss leaving a 16" (41 cm) end.

FINISHING
Thread tapestry needle with end and work blanket stitch across bound off stitches to reinforce edge *(Figs. 1a & b, page 34)*. Weave end to center of short edge. ★ Remove tapestry needle and thread beading needle with end. Pass through spacer bead, through toggle, then back through spacer bead allowing $1/4$" (6 mm) slack on each side of toggle. Remove beading needle and thread tapestry needle with end. Knot securely at center of short edge. Repeat from ★ once **more** taking care not to catch previous floss when passing through spacer bead. Cut floss leaving a $1/16$" (1.5 mm) end. Anchor end with matching sewing thread. Apply clear nail polish to end and tuck end inside spacer bead.

Repeat for second end.

PEARL ELEGANCE CUFF

Shown on front cover

Skill Level: ■■□□ **EASY**

Finished Size: 1½" (4 cm) wide x 7¼" (18.5 cm) long (including toggle); Bracelet will stretch to fit 7¼"-7¾" wrist (18.5-20 cm)

MATERIALS

Polyester embroidery floss, 8¾ yards (8 meters) - 3 skeins
Straight knitting needles, size 2 (2.75 mm)
Pearl seed beads - 196
Clear seed beads - 45
Toggle clasp set
Blunt tapestry needle
Beading needle
Sewing needle and thread to match floss
Clear nail polish

To lengthen or shorten by ³⁄₈" (1 cm), increase or decrease the number of pearl beads strung in increments of 6.

Bracelet

String Beads: Using beading needle, string 75 pearl beads onto floss.

Leaving a 48" (122 cm) end, cast on 9 sts.

Rows 1-4: Knit across.

Row 5 (Wrong side)**:** K3, WYB slide bead up, ★ K1, WYB slide bead up; repeat from ★ across to last 3 sts, K3: 4 beads.

Rows 6-8: Knit across.

Rows 9-12: Repeat Rows 5-8.

Row 13: K2, WYB slide bead up, ★ K1, WYB slide bead up; repeat from ★ across to last 2 sts, K2: 6 beads.

Rows 14-16: Knit across.

Repeat Rows 13-16 for pattern until you reach the end of your floss, ending by working Row 14. String 31 pearl beads onto second strand of floss. With first floss, knit to the middle of the row, join second skein and knit across *(see Joining New Floss, page 3)*.

Beginning with Row 16, continue in pattern until Bracelet measures approximately 5½" (14 cm) from cast on edge or 2" (5 cm) less than desired finished length, ending by working Row 16.

Next 8 Rows: Repeat Rows 5-12.

Bind off all sts. Cut floss leaving a 24" (61 cm) end.

FINISHING

Thread tapestry needle with long cast on end and work blanket stitch at corner for reinforcement *(Figs. 1a & b, page 34)*. Change to beading needle and string 135 edging beads as follows: ★ string 2 pearl beads, string 1 clear bead; repeat from ★ until all beads are strung. Pull the beads tight and tie an overhand knot to keep them taut.

Position the beaded end around the edge of the Bracelet. Thread tapestry needle with a 36" (91.5 cm) length of floss. Sew the beaded tail to the Bracelet's edge with overhand stitches, bringing the needle up and down between each bead, working around the entire Bracelet. Loosen knot and remove any unused beads from beaded end. Join ends neatly and secure tightly with a knot. Weave the end of the sewing floss to the Bracelet. Cut floss leaving a ¹⁄₁₆" (1.5 mm) end.

Thread tapestry needle with cast on end and weave to center of short end. ★ Remove tapestry needle and thread beading needle with end. Thread end through toggle, allowing ¼" (6 mm) slack on each side of toggle. Remove beading needle and thread tapestry needle with end. Knot securely at center of short edge. Repeat from ★ once **more**. Cut floss leaving a ¹⁄₁₆" (1.5 mm) end. Anchor end with matching sewing thread. Apply clear nail polish to end.

Instructions continued on page 28.

FOREST WHISPERS

Shown on page 29

Skill Level: ■■□□ **EASY**

Finished Size: 1" (2.5 cm) wide x $7^1/_2$" (19 cm) long (including toggle); Bracelet will stretch to fit $7^1/_4$-$7^3/_4$" wrist (18.5-20 cm)

MATERIALS
Polyester embroidery floss, $8^3/_4$ yards (8 meters)
- 1 skein
Straight knitting needles, size 2 (2.75 mm)
Resin shell beads - 10
8 mm Glass beads - 10
4 mm Glass beads - 10
6 mm Flat gemstones - 6
Metal word charms - 5
Spacer beads - 2
Toggle clasp set
Blunt tapestry needle
Beading needle
Sewing needle and thread to match floss
Clear nail polish

To lengthen or shorten by $^3/_4$" (2 cm), increase or decrease one bead at each end of strand to maintain symmetry. Repeat Rows 3 and 4 once more or less at the beginning and end of the pattern for each bead added or removed.

Bracelet
String Beads: Using beading needle, string 41 beads onto floss as follows:

flat gemstone
8 mm bead
resin shell bead
8 mm bead
resin shell bead
4 mm bead
word charm
4 mm bead
flat gemstone
8 mm bead
resin shell bead
8 mm bead
resin shell bead
4 mm bead
word charm
4 mm bead
flat gemstone
8 mm bead
resin shell bead
4 mm bead
word charm
4 mm bead
resin shell bead
8 mm bead
flat gemstone
4 mm bead
word charm
4 mm bead
resin shell bead
8 mm bead
resin shell bead
8 mm bead
flat gemstone
4 mm bead
word charm
4 mm bead
resin shell bead
8 mm bead
resin shell bead
8 mm bead
flat gemstone

FOREST WHISPERS

Continued from page 27.

Leaving a 16" (41 cm) end, cast on 3 sts.

Rows 1 and 2: Knit across.

Row 3 (Right side)**:** K1, WYF slide bead up, P1, K1.

Row 4: Knit across.

Row 5: K2, WYF slide bead up, P1.

Row 6: Knit across.

Rows 7-12: Repeat Rows 3-6 once, then repeat Rows 3 and 4 once **more**.

Row 13: K2, WYF slide 3 beads up, P1.

Row 14: Knit across.

Rows 15-26: Repeat Rows 3-14.

Rows 27-32: Repeat Rows 3-6 once, then repeat Rows 3 and 4 once **more**.

Row 33: K2, WYF slide 3 beads up, P1.

Row 34: Knit across.

Rows 35-40: Repeat Rows 3-6 once, then repeat Rows 3 and 4 once **more**.

Row 41: K2, WYF slide 3 beads up, P1.

Row 42: Knit across.

Rows 43-52: Repeat Rows 3-6 twice, then repeat Rows 3 and 4 once **more**.

Rows 53 and 54: Repeat Rows 13 and 14.

Rows 55-64: Repeat Rows 3-6 twice, then repeat Rows 3 and 4 once **more**.

Bind off all sts. Cut floss leaving a 16" (41 cm) end.

FINISHING

Thread tapestry needle with end and work blanket stitch across bound off stitches to reinforce edge **(Figs. 1a & b, page 34)**. Weave end to center of short edge. ★ Remove tapestry needle and thread beading needle with end. Pass through spacer bead, through toggle, then back through spacer bead allowing $1/4$" (6 mm) slack on each side of toggle. Remove beading needle and thread tapestry needle with end. Knot securely at center of short edge. Repeat from ★ once **more** taking care not to catch previous floss when passing through spacer bead. Cut floss leaving a $1/16$" (1.5 mm) end. Anchor end with matching sewing thread. Apply clear nail polish to end and tuck end inside spacer bead.

Repeat for second end.

PEARL ELEGANCE CUFF

Continued from page 26.

Thread tapestry needle with bind off end and weave through sts to center of bound off edge. Attach second end of toggle in same manner.

Pattern Variations: This Bracelet can be worked with any odd number of sts. For a narrower Bracelet cast on 7 sts and adjust number of beads accordingly; for a wider Bracelet, cast on 11 or 13 sts.

CARIBE DAZZLE

Skill Level: ■■□□ **EASY**

Finished Size: 1¼" (3 cm) wide x 7½" (19 cm) long (including toggle); Bracelet will stretch to fit 7½"-7¾" wrist (19-20 cm)

MATERIALS
Polyester embroidery floss, 8¾ yards (8 meters) - 3 skeins
Straight knitting needles, size 2 (2.75 mm)
Crochet hook, size E (3.5 mm)
6/0 mixed glass seed beads - 153
6/0 solid seed beads - 56
10 mm shell disk beads - 30
6/0 ceramic tube beads (9 mm length) - 9
Toggle clasp set
Blunt tapestry needle
Beading needle
Sewing needle and thread to match floss
Clear nail polish

Bracelet
MIXED BEAD STRAND (Make 2)
String Beads: Using beading needle, string 56 mixed seed beads onto floss.

Leaving a 16" (41 cm) end, cast on 2 sts.

Rows 1 and 2: Knit across.

Row 3: K1, WYF slide bead up, P1.

Repeat Row 3 for pattern until strand measures approximately 6¾" (17 cm) from cast on edge, or 1¾" (4.5 cm) less than desired finished length.

Last Row: Knit across.

Bind off all sts. Cut floss leaving a 16" (41 cm) end.

SOLID BEAD STRAND
Using solid seed beads, work same as Mixed Bead Strand.

CHAIN STRAND
String Beads: Using beading needle, string one mixed seed bead, ★ string three 10 mm disk beads, string one mixed seed bead; repeat from ★ 9 times **more**.

Using crochet hook and leaving a 16" (41 cm) end, ★ slide bead up, ch 1; repeat from ★ until strand measures same as previous strands; finish off.

Cut floss leaving a 16" (41 cm) end.

PLAIN STRAND
Leaving a 16" (41 cm) end, tie an overhand knot in floss.

String Beads: Using beading needle, string 3 mixed seed beads, ★ string one 9 mm tube bead, string 3 mixed seed beads; repeat from ★ 8 times **more**. Pull the beads tight and tie an overhand knot to keep them taut.

Cut floss leaving a 16" (41 cm) end.

FINISHING
FIRST END
Holding all ends together evenly, tie an overhand knot snugly against the end of all strands. Using beading needle, thread the ends through one end of toggle. Allowing ¼" (6 mm) slack on each side of toggle, tie a second overhand knot. Remove beading needle and thread tapestry needle with end, then securely knot the ends to the strands below the overhand knot. Cut floss leaving ¹⁄₁₆" (1.5 mm) ends. Anchor ends with matching sewing thread. Apply clear nail polish to ends and overhand knots.

SECOND END
Gather remaining tails on second end of Bracelet, twist the beaded strands loosely together. Tie an overhand knot flush against the twisted strands and finish same as First End.

OCEAN BREEZE

Skill Level: ⬛⬛⬜⬜ **EASY**

Finished Size: 1¼" (3 cm) wide x 7½" (19 cm) long (including toggle); Bracelet will stretch to fit 7½-7¾" wrist (18.5-20 cm)

MATERIALS
Polyester embroidery floss, 8¾ yards (8 meters)
  - 1 skein
Straight knitting needles, size 2 (2.75 mm)
6 mm Bone beads - 2
4 mm Beads - 16
4 mm Flat discs - 14
Resin shell beads - 10
Shell rings - 7
10 mm Gemstone beads - 4
Metal word rings - 4
Metal word charms - 4
Spacer beads - 2
Toggle clasp set
Blunt tapestry needle
Beading needle
Sewing needle and thread to match floss
Clear nail polish

To lengthen or shorten by ½" (12 mm), remove ending bone bead, increase or decrease the number of beads strung in increments of 4, then replace bone bead at end of sequence.

Bracelet
String Beads: Using beading needle, string 61 beads onto floss as follows:

bone bead
4 mm bead
word ring
4 mm bead
resin shell bead
4 mm flat disc
shell ring
4 mm flat disc
resin shell bead
4 mm bead
word charm
4 mm bead
gemstone bead
4 mm flat disc
shell ring
4 mm flat disc
resin shell bead
4 mm bead
word ring
4 mm bead
resin shell bead
4 mm flat disc
shell ring
4 mm flat disc
gemstone bead
4 mm bead
word charm
4 mm bead
resin shell bead
4 mm flat disc
shell ring
4 mm flat disc
resin shell bead
4 mm bead
word charm
4 mm bead
gemstone bead
4 mm flat disc
shell ring
4 mm flat disc
resin shell bead
4 mm bead
word ring
4 mm bead
resin shell bead
4 mm flat disc
shell ring
4 mm flat disc
gemstone bead
4 mm bead
word charm
4 mm bead
resin shell bead
4 mm flat disc
shell ring
4 mm flat disc
resin shell bead
4 mm bead
word ring
4 mm bead
bone bead

...aving a 16" (41 cm) end, cast on 3 sts.

...1 and 2: Knit across.

...Right side): K1, WYF slide bead up, P1, K1.

...it across.

...WYF slide 3 beads up, P1: 3 beads.

...t across.

Repeat Rows 3-6 for pattern until all beads have been used and Bracelet measures approximately 6" (15 cm) from cast on edge or 1¹/₂" (4 cm) less than desired finished length, ending by working Row 4.

Bind off all sts. Cut floss leaving a 16" (41 cm) end.

FINISHING
Complete same as Forest Whispers, page 28.

GENERAL INSTRUCTIONS

ABBREVIATIONS

ch(s)	chain(s)
cm	centimeters
K	knit
mm	millimeters
P	purl
st(s)	stitch(es)
WYB	with yarn in back
WYF	with yarn in front

★ — work instructions following ★ as many **more** times as indicated in addition to the first time.

( ) — contains explanatory remarks.

colon (:) — the number given after a colon at the end of a row denotes the number of beads you should have on that row.

GAUGE

The instructions in this leaflet are written for 6-ply polyester metallic embroidery floss. Gauge is not of great importance; the Bracelets can be adjusted to your wrist size without changing the overall effect by following the individual project instructions.

BLANKET STITCH

Come up at 1; go in at 2, leaving a small loop. Come up again at 3 directly below 2 and in line with 1 while holding floss under needle with thumb **(Fig. 1a)**. Pull floss through. Repeat across edge **(Fig. 1b)**.

Fig. 1a

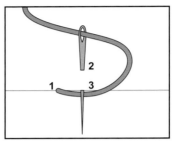

Fig. 1b

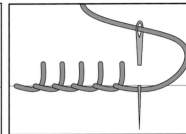

WEAVING SEAMS

With the right side of Bracelet facing you and edges even, sew through both sides once to secure the seam. Insert the needle under the bar between the first and second stitches on the row and pull the floss through **(Fig. 2)**. Insert the needle under the next bar on the second side. Repeat from side to side, being careful to match rows.

Fig. 2

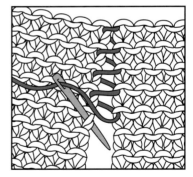

KNIT TERMINOLOGY	
UNITED STATES	**INTERNATIONAL**
gauge =	tension
bind off =	cast off
yarn over (YO) =	yarn forward (yfwd) **or** yarn around needle (yrn)

KNITTING NEEDLES																
U.S.	0	1	2	3	4	5	6	7	8	9	10	10½	11	13	15	17
U.K.	13	12	11	10	9	8	7	6	5	4	3	2	1	00	000	---
Metric - mm	2	2.25	2.75	3.25	3.5	3.75	4	4.5	5	5.5	6	6.5	8	9	10	12.75

■□□□ **BEGINNER**	Projects for first-time knitters using basic knit and purl stitches. Minimal shaping.
■■□□ **EASY**	Projects using basic stitches, repetitive stitch patterns, simple color changes, and simple shaping and finishing.
■■■□ **INTERMEDIATE**	Projects with a variety of stitches, such as basic cables and lace, simple intarsia, double-pointed needles and knitting in the round needle techniques, mid-level shaping and finishing.
■■■■ **EXPERIENCED**	Projects using advanced techniques and stitches, such as short rows, fair isle, more intricate intarsia, cables, lace patterns, and numerous color changes.

PROJECT INFORMATION

Each Bracelet in this leaflet was made using DMC Light Effects, Art. 317W polyester metallic embroidery floss.
Any brand of 6-ply metallic floss may be used.
For your convenience, listed below are the specific floss colors and beads used to create our photography models.

BEADS GALORE
Floss
Antique Effects #E310 black
Beads
A Touch of Class
Round Swirl Design and/or Animal Print
12 PC-mix 8 mm #32794
Dress it Up Beads
Multi-color large seed beads #1-2612

CARIBE DAZZLE
Floss
Jewel Effects # E3849 aqua
Beads
Dress it Up Beads
Tiny Beads #2867 aqua
Blue Moon Beads
#BM45214 Green Frost
Bead Heaven
Sapphire Enamel tube bead spacers
10 mm Mother of Pearl Tinted Aqua disc bead shells

CRYSTAL LAKE
Floss
Precious Metal Effects #E168 light silver
Beads
Bead Heaven
6 mm crystal beads #82483
TOHO Treasure Beads
4 mm Silver lined clear cube beads #1955-407

DAZZLE BRAID
Floss
Precious Metal Effects #E677 light gold
Antique Effects #E415 silver
Beads
Blue Moon Beads
#BM51705 gold
TOHO Treasure Beads
4 mm Cube beads #1955-407 silver-lined clear

FIRE AND ICE
Floss
Antique Effects #E898 brown
Beads
Dress it Up Beads
6 mm Special Effects crystal/copper
6 mm Clear/white crystal

FOREST WHISPERS
Floss
Precious Metal Effects #E168 light silver
Beads
Blue Moon Beads Natural Elegance
Flat Gemstones
Resin Shells
8 mm Glass beads
4 mm Glass beads
Word charms

GOLDEN SEA
Floss
Precious Metal Effects #E677 light gold
Beads
Assorted 4-6 mm crystals and seed beads in gold,
aqua, sea green, light blue, light pink and lavender

HOT PASTEL GUM DROPS

Floss
> Precious Metal Effects #E301 copper

Beads
> Assorted 6-10 mm glass beads in bright red, pink, green, gold, aqua, mixed with a few lighter pastel color beads

OCEAN BREEZE

Floss
> Antique Effects #E436 light brown

Beads
> Blue Moon Beads Natural Elegance
> > 6 mm Flowered bone beads
> > 10 mm Gemstone beads
> > Resin marbled tan shell beads
> > Word rings
> > Word charms
> > 4 mm Beads
> > 4 mm Flat round disc beads
> > Shell rings

PEARL ELEGANCE CUFF

Floss
> Precious Metal Effects #E677 light gold

Beads
> Beader's Paradise
> > Super white pearl seed beads
> > Silver-lined clear seed beads

PINK ICE CUFF

Floss
> Precious Metal Effects #E168 light silver

Beads
> Assorted 4-10 mm sizes and shapes of crystal glass beads with aura borealis finish and/or iridescent finishing in light pink, rose and clear
> Frosted glass beads in light pink, medium pink, rose, and clear
> Pink glass leaf beads

PURPLE PASSION BANGLE

Floss
> Jewel Effects #E155 lavender

Beads
> Beader's Paradise
> > Amethyst mix seed beads

RAINBOW

Floss
> Precious Metal Effects #E301 copper

Beads
> Assorted 4-10 mm glass beads in rainbow colors

TWILIGHT

Floss
> Antique Effects #E310 black

Beads
> Assorted 4-6 mm crystals and seed beads in black, violet, hot pink, aqua, gold, clear, pearl white, sea green, olive green, light pink, and lavender

YOUR CHOICE

Floss
> Precious Metal Effects #E168 light silver

Beads
> Assorted sizes and shapes of 4-10 mm Black, white, clear and red beads

Production Team: Editor – Joan Beebe; Graphic Artist - Liz Field; Photo Stylist - Sonya Daniel; and Photographer - Ken West.

For digital downloads of Leisure Arts' best-selling designs, visit http://www.leisureartslibrary.com